I0054114

Scott Howard's Tips on Becoming a Highly Paid Public Speaker

Tips on Overcoming the Fear of Speaking, Preparing and Presenting Your Speech and Getting Hired to Speak

Richard G Lowe, Jr

Scott Howard's Tips on Becoming a Highly Paid Public Speaker

Tips on Overcoming the Fear of Speaking, Preparing and
Presenting Your Speech and Getting Hired to Speak

Interviews with Influencers Series #1

Published by The Writing King
www.thewritingking.com

Scott Howard's Tips on Becoming a Highly Paid Public Speaker

Copyright © 2016 by Richard G Lowe, Jr.

All rights reserved. No part of this publication may be reproduced, stored in a retrieval system, or transmitted by any means – electronic, mechanical, photographic (photocopying), recording, or otherwise – without prior permission in writing from the author.

Although every precaution has been taken to verify the accuracy of the information contained herein, the author and publisher assume no responsibility for any errors or omissions. No liability is assumed for damages that may result from the use of information contained within.

Trademarked names appear throughout this book. Rather than use a trademark symbol with every occurrence of a trademarked name, names are used in an editorial fashion, with no intention of infringement of the respective owner's trademark.

Cover Artist: theamateurzone

ASIN: B01EIMN17Y
ISBN: 978-1-943517-90-9 (Hardcover)
ISBN: 978-1-943517-24-4 (Paperback)
ISBN: 978-1-943517-23-7 (eBook)

.

Table of Contents

A Special Note about how this book was created............................ 3

Introduction 1

Background... 3

How Did You Feel the First Time You Spoke for Pay?.............. 11

What is the First Skill Every Public Speaker Needs?.................. 15

What is the Second Skill Every Public Speaker Needs to Know? 19

What is the Third Skill a Public Speaker Should Work on?.. 23

Are There Any Other Skills Needed to Speak in Public?............. 27

Do You Have Any Recommendations for Tools?......................... 29

Where do You See Public Speakers Wasting Time When They're Speaking?... 33

How Important is Good Grammar in Speaking? 45

What About Umms and Ahhs and Sort of's, All the Little Stop Gap Words?... 49

How Important Are Props in Public Speaking?......................... 51

How Would You Develop a Trademark Kind of Speaking Pattern? 53

How Would You Handle an Audience That Turns Out to be a Little Hostile? 57

Are There any Books You Would Recommend to Our Audience and Why?... 61

In Closing, Is There Anything You Want to Add?...................... 65

Closing... 67

Creatively Inspiring' Scott Howard...................................... 71

About the Author 73

Books by Richard G Lowe Jr. 77

Additional Resources.. 83

Premium Writing Services... 85

A Special Note about how this book was created

Dear reader,

Thank you for buying your copy of *Scott Howard's Tips on Becoming a Highly Paid Public Speaker*.

This book will teach you critical public speaking skills, tools, techniques and more that every speaker needs to understand and apply.

This book was transcribed from a live interview.

That's why it reads as a conversation rather than a traditional "book" that talks "at" you.

Get ready to take your public speaking to the next level so you can understand how to become a highly paid public speaker.

Sincerely,

Scott Howard

Introduction

Richard Lowe (RL): Hi everyone and welcome to the *Interviews with Influencers* e-book series.

(Today's interview is sponsored by **Scott Howard's website at MyScottArt.com and ArtsyAntBook.com**. Check out Scott Howard's websites for more information.)

The title of today's interview is **"Scott Howard's Tips on Becoming a Highly Paid Public Speaker."**

My name is Richard Lowe and today I'm speaking with **public speaking** expert **Scott Howard** about the critical skills every public speaker needs to **learn to be a successful public speaker, make the right impression on their audience and get the best results**.

Welcome, **Scott Howard**.

Scott Howard (SH): Hi Richard.

RL: Scott is a hands-on expert on the subject of **public speaking**, and has graciously consented to this interview to share with us the skills every **public speaker** can and must develop in order to know how to **speak effectively market yourself and your brand**.

Scott, thank you again for joining us on this live interview.

Let's jump right in.

Background

SH: Alright, thank you for having me here.

RL: My first set of questions is about your background, and experience in the field of public speaking. So that public speakers in our audience can understand who you are, how you developed the skills, and how you can relate to where they are right now.

We'll jump right into the major skills all public speakers need with so they can set themselves up for success. Could you tell us a little about yourself regarding background, education, and experience in public speaking?

SH: My true career background was in graphic design and illustration, taking and majoring in art in college and minoring in psychology, one of the electives I took was public speaking.

Now, for me talking about, I'm ashamed to admit it, almost 40 years ago, I got all A's in that course, and through that, I found that it actually helped my career. Just taking those classes in college helped me with things like stepping up in college and being able to be out front of the homecoming pageant, and helped to be on stage for different events.

I got involved in different business as I grew, and even as a graphic designer, presentation skills. Whether you're presenting at an ad agency to clients or speaking to your own executors at a company, or presenting an idea to somebody, I found that those public speaking skills helped me along.

There was one company I was with in the nineties, and it was a software company, and about every other month our marketing department would present new software to a sales force of 200 people, and we would put on a big presentation, almost like an act. That, oddly enough, helped to encourage my public speaking skills.

Finally, in mid-2000's, I started working on a children's book, and I was going to these seminars where they were saying that if you want to become a successful author, you should also become a competent speaker.

So I started asking where do you go to do that? The answer that came to me was Toastmasters, so I joined the Toastmasters group, and I went into it with the idea that it wasn't a matter of getting over a fear of speaking, it was wanting to become a good, competent speaker.

It was wanting to be able to present my book and myself and to stand up on stage and be able to be motivational and inspirational, and to do it without umms and errs and ahhs and nervousness, and doubts about what I was speaking about, and to be able to organize my speaking.

I can say, from there, that I developed many of those skills and went beyond that. Toastmasters taught other things: leadership skills and communication skills that have helped me in business relationships and network connections, and other things that have come about that I didn't even foresee, so the combination of all of those things; my education, the training, the businesses

I've been in, to write a book and end up in Toastmasters and now to be a paid professional speaker; has been an unexpected journey.

It's all been for me kind of a sideline of something that came about from something else I was doing, and it actually makes me wish that I had really focused on becoming a professional speaker 40 years ago when I was in college and already going that direction.

RL: I understand. What kind of things have you done, or experiences have you had in public speaking, that are relevant to our audience? To learn how to speak in public?

SH: Well, it would depend a lot on who that audience is, and what the direction is that they are going in. I would honestly say that if we're talking about beginners, somebody that's relatively new, join something like Toastmasters.

There is where you're going to learn the fundamentals of public speaking. I often like to tell people, learn from the best, study the best, and discover, depending on what your niche is.

Let's say you would like to become a motivational or inspirational speaker. Look at speakers like Anthony Robbins or Jack Canfield of the Chicken Soup for the Soul books, or watch some of the videos of Wayne Dyer when he's on stage, any of the leadership speakers that are out there, business leaders, and study them and see how they do.

Get books and listen to audiobooks and watch videos on YouTube of professional speakers and championship speakers.

Les Brown is a good example of somebody who was once in radio and became a professional speaker, and study them. But then, take that and become your best you.

The objective is not to become like Les Brown or Jack Canfield or Wayne Dyer; it is to study them and learn from them and see what makes them great, and then you take your personality and bring that to the stage.

So, that would be probably the greatest thing I could say to anybody. Study the best and then develop your own personality. You're creating a perception of who you are when you're up on stage in front of people.

RL: Okay, how do you develop the "you" you're talking about?

SH: It takes a little work and a little effort. I can only give my example of how it went for me. After a few years in Toastmasters and I was becoming confident at speaking and getting up and telling stories and putting it out there, but when it finally came to how can I get paid as a speaker, it came down to now it's time for me to create a website.

To create an image of who I am and who's going to hire me, and what am I going to speak on, and it's finding my niche.

Well, over time I realized I had a couple of different things. One, my background was in art, in creativity.

Next, I'm partly recognized by people as a children's book author and an illustrator, and then third what I really like to speak about is motivational, inspirational.

I like storytelling for kids, and I like empowering people of all ages. I like encouraging them to believe in themselves and chase their dreams, so how do I find my niche in that?

I came up with a tagline that says "creatively inspiring," and that 'creatively' goes along with the art, the children's books, and the 'inspiring' goes along with the motivational.

It took me several months of working on my website and trying to write out notes of what is my niche and who am I trying to appeal to, who is my audience before I even came up with that tagline.

So I think for each person, you have to look inside first at what do you want to speak about, how do you want to be seen, who is the audience that you're going to appeal to, and narrow that down and really find your niche.

And so, if that answers your question I think that's all I'm going to say.

It comes down to an individual thing. One person may be strong at leadership skills, and another it might be business management, so one person's audience could be speaking to sales organizations, and another it might be executives in business, and another it might be a general audience.

One person might be good at speaking to the different Rotary clubs and the Knights of Columbus, and Kiwanis, while somebody else will be out speaking to women's groups empowering women, or talking to the parent-teacher associations so, it's again finding that niche that you feel you have the most knowledge of or background in or experience in or would like to talk about, and really work on that niche.

How Did You Feel the First Time You Spoke for Pay?

SH: Hmm. The first experiences of getting paid were not paid all that much, and getting paid in speaking can have a number of different ways of making that happen.

I would actually say my first getting paid was not so much earning a paycheck for it as much as being told that I could sell my books or things on the side.

So, you're actually taking the opportunity to speak to get the experience, but you're asking ahead of time can I bring along my books and sell them from the back of the room or promote them from the stage, and when you do that, if you promote well then you can actually make a pretty good paycheck on selling whatever products you have.

I know there are speakers who have DVDs and CDs they sell as well; some have whole packages and they can fill a table with their products. So, that works to help getting paid while you're developing.

To actually get paid I would say one of the big surprises, and I learned this by becoming a member of the National Speaker Association; they like to say that they don't want to talk about money and pricing; but it was discovering that the price to get paid as a speaker is actually higher than I expected, and one of the things I learned was when asked what do you charge for speaking, is to almost throw it back at them and say, well I have a couple of different packages I can offer.

Do you just want a keynote speaker, would you want me to be able to teach workshops, will I be able to bring my books or CDs with me to sell them, and you're building up a package, and then say, so tell me, what is your budget?

And I found oftentimes the budget people were planning to pay me was a whole lot higher than what I was actually planning to charge them. So, that would be my recommendation there.

And, these days I kind of hate to even put a number out there, but most competent speakers who've got at least a few good years of experience, have worked in Toastmasters and learning to deliver their message, even when they're just getting out and getting paid speaking, it's not uncommon to make $2500 or $3000 for a speech, for a keynote speech that's say an hour and a half long.

The thing you have to realize when you say that is you're not really getting paid for an hour and a half; you're also getting paid for all the preparation that you're going to put into getting ready for that presentation before you get there.

If you're going to be speaking out of town, the company will be paying for your travels; they'll pay for your hotel as well, so there's a lot more to it than just how do you get paid.

But I will say that when you start getting paid, it's a pretty good feeling. There's almost this thing inside where you say, wow am I really worth this? And there's a little bit of that self-doubt, and just don't let yourself doubt yourself too much.

Believe that if they're willing to pay you, then you're worth it.

What is the First Skill Every Public Speaker Needs?

SH: The first skill... A number of things run through my mind, and the first I want to say is the desire to want to speak.

In Toastmasters, I will say that the majority of people who joined Toastmasters joined because they wanted to get over their fear of speaking. It's something they'd either never thought of until a certain recent time or something they've always thought of and were deathly afraid of doing, and for the majority of people doing Toastmasters, probably over half to three-quarters, that's the reason they're joining.

There are the few of us who actually join with the idea of actually wanting to improve speaking skills and communication skills. Some of them come in because they're suddenly in a job where they're going to have to give presentations or stand up in a board room and speak, and the idea of it scares the heck out of them.

So, they're just trying to develop that new skill. So, I would say developing some comfort and confidence is probably an important part. But, that still has to come in some part with the desire and inclination to do it. If you think that you'll never see yourself as a speaker, then you'll never be a speaker, just like anything else.

RL: That's good. So how do you develop that?

SH: Again, for me it's finding a way to do it. I've heard the term stage time many times.

There are a lot of professional speakers and championship speakers who say stage time stage time stage time, it's getting practice doing it.

It's pretty much like doing anything else. None of us are born speaking, none of us are born writers or artists. We might have something inside of us that drives us towards that, that we feel we have this skill, this talent, something that shows up in grade school, but we have to develop it.

We don't learn to be doctors or lawyers or engineers or anything else just by saying, I want to be that and you're it. You have to develop a skill, and you have to learn how that business is run.

So, to me one of the best places to get those fundamental skills is Toastmasters, and I know there are some other groups out there; there are a lot of workshops and speaking groups that go around and run seminars and offer to help people become better speakers, to be able to sell from the stage, but most of those are for people who already have the fundamentals.

There's not much beyond Toastmasters that's going to teach the fundamentals, and I'm gonna say again that Toastmasters is not the end all. If you want to really become a professional speaker, you'll still have to go beyond that organization.

But to get involved and get those basics right there, to learn how to tell a story, how to not have umms and errs and ahhs, to learn how to organize a speech, to learn how to get to the point, how to go from telling a story to giving the message of that story and presenting it, and to learn how to use visual aids and PowerPoint slides comfortably and without standing with your back to the audience or looking at the slides yourself, those are the fundamentals of speaking.

So again I recommend Toastmasters, and to anybody who is a beginner I recommend Toastmasters as a place to start, and there are Toastmasters organizations in almost any city, and just about any state, and not just in the States but in countries all over the world. But that would be the place to start.

Get into something like that for a two or three years and by then you'll be ready to move on in whatever individual direction you want to go in. So that would be my recommendation, my suggestion.

What is the Second Skill Every Public Speaker Needs to Know?

SH: I think one of the keys to speaking is storytelling. If you can open with a story; and this goes back to your opening.

When you have an opening, how you get introduced, and you come up to a stage, within a matter of seconds that audience is going to make a decision about you. They're going to see how you're dressed, how you present yourself. Do you look nervous? Are you dressed professionally? Is this a professional person? And, they're going to make a decision.

People do that automatically; it's like judgment. It seems to happen automatically in people. Within a minute, your audience is going to be deciding whether they want to listen to you or not.

So, how do you come up and make an authority of yourself? You've been asked to come in and speak about traffic on the roads. You might not know a lot about traffic, but let's say somehow you've been asked to do that.

So, the best way to grab that audience's attention right off the bat is to come up and tell a story, generally something from your experience. And if you've got a story that's amusing or entertaining, exciting, suspenseful, and you can grab that audience's attention, it can do two things.

One, the audience can relate to you. If you've got empathy, they can relate to the empathy. If you've got something sad, and it's a story about somebody you knew in a car accident, they can relate because they've had somebody they know in a car accident.

If you've got something humorous that happened on the road, they can relate. If you want to talk about a tire blowing out, and you're ending up on the side of the road, and the police officer who came and wanted to write you a ticket, you can grab their attention with that.

The other thing that storytelling can do is that it can make you appear as an authority to that audience within a very short matter of time.

Let's say, you're an author, and you've written science fiction books, but you've just come out with these books, and the audience doesn't know you. So, how do you come up and present yourself as an authority as a science fiction writer?

Well, the best thing to do would be to come in and start telling a story that influenced you or inspired you as a child. Let's say, when I was a kid, I read this book, and this book got my attention. It was the story of a girl who fell down a hole, and into a whole different dimension, a world of unbelievable characters and things happening.

Right away, that audience is paying attention to what you've got to say, and it's putting you in as an authority who not only had influences as a child, but helped to create who you are as an adult, and the audience is relating to you.

So, I would say that's the second key to being a great speaker is storytelling, and tell a story, give a message. Tell a story, give a message, tell a story, give a message. You can open your speech with a big story, you can have a story in the middle, and you can end your speech with a story that relates to what you opened with, and you've created a great speech.

What is the Third Skill a Public Speaker Should Work on?

SH: The third skill. A lot of skills here. [laughter].

I'm going to say confidence. It's something in yourself that's how you present yourself. It is, there's a confidence that comes partly from being onstage.

That can make some people so nervous and make them lack confidence, but it goes along with seeing yourself. It's how you see yourself.

When you can get to a point where, it's not that you don't care what other people think about you, but you realize that not everybody in the world is going to like you, but you like you, and you can see yourself as a leader.

As somebody who has a message that other people might want to hear, could learn from, could improve from, could entertain, then that perception of how you see yourself will also come out to your audience.

Your audience will see you that way. So, I would say it's confidence, and seeing yourself as a leader, and seeing yourself as having something valuable to share with other people.

Whether it's entertaining, fun, important, educational, informative, how you see yourself and the message you have to give, I would say, would probably be the third skill. And again, this is improvisational. Later on, I may think, wow I should've said this, but for right now that's what I'm thinking.

RL: And how do you develop that?

SH: As I said, stage time. It's doing it, it's practice, it's like anything else. If somebody offered you a job as a waiter in a nice restaurant, and you'd never waited tables, how would you develop it?

You'd develop it by going and doing it and learning where things are. Here's how the computer system works, here's your customers, you're learning these skills.

If you're going to work as a cashier at a grocery store, you're going to develop certain skills, but you're going to learn it by doing it.

You can go to school, you can learn, and Toastmasters is going to teach you some of that, and you're going to have leadership skills, but there's nothing better than actual on the job experience.

Sometimes without any kind of background in it, getting that experience is the hardest part, but that's where something like Toastmasters or like going to a community college, getting those introductory speaking skills, is going to give you those first steps.

That's all I would say; find a way to get the introductions and get the experience, and doing it. To get up in front of people; there's nothing better, nothing more valuable.

And something like Toastmasters where you have people who've been doing it a long time and who can evaluate you and give you tips and clues along the way is going to help you even more.

Very similarly, I'd say in a public speaking class in a community college, you will have a teacher there, and you'll have other students who'll be helping to give evaluations of each other, and help each other improve and get better.

So, again, that would be what I would offer. Something like that as a place to start. And it's just stage time, stage time, stage time.

RL: So you'd offer the same advice for overcoming stage fright?

SH: Pretty much, yeah. You learn by doing it. So, that would be it. One thing I would add to that is I've heard it said that the best speakers are those who can evaluate other speakers.

So, getting involved in a place in a way where you're learning these fundamentals, and how to be able to help others with those fundamentals, is going to help you become better along the way as well.

The more that you learn how to listen; listening is a big part, how to listen for pronunciation, language, the ability to hear someone say ahh, and umms and uhhs, and fill-in language, and be able to recognize that, and watch for certain gestures and body language, and the more you develop those skills to see it in other people, the more you're going to improve on that yourself.

And the more you're able to help somebody else to say, you're still pacing a bit when you're up there, it comes out of your nervousness, or you have this way of, let's say, language. You use the word 'like' and 'you know' a lot in your language.

Well, to the average person, in conversation they won't even novice it, it's just part of conversation, but when you're learning the fundamentals of speaking you become aware of it, and the more you become aware of it and the more you're able to help others, the better you're going to become as a speaker yourself, and the more you're going to be perceived as a leader in that field.

Are There Any Other Skills Needed to Speak in Public?

SH: It helps to be socially active. I don't know that I want to say socially outgoing. I've seen a lot of people who were actually kind of on the shy side who can develop great speaking skills, same thing like acting.

You've heard of some big name actors who, socially, in public, their social skills aren't great, but when they get on stage or they're in front of a camera, they're able to take on a different personality.

However, when it comes to speaking, I would just say that those social skills; learning to smile, to help others, that's probably a big part, it's being able to walk into a room and not only say that this room is about me and how can I impress others, but what can I do for you?

I'm a member of a business organization called CEO Space, and they have a phrase that when you meet somebody, you say, "hi, what's your name, what do you do, and how can I help you?" What are you looking for?

And, it goes along with the Dale Carnegie "How to Win Friends and Influence People" thing, that instead of being ready to talk about yourself, it's being ready to talk about the other person.

When you're going to be the public speaker at an event, get there a half an hour or an hour early, and to be able to walk around and talk to people and socialize with them, and ask them, "What are they looking for? What are your needs?" can actually give you some tips into what you can add into your speaking when you are presenting.

I would say that, just, social skills and being able to talk and give attention to other people, and find out what their needs are and how you can help them, it's to serve others, is a very valuable skill that will help in speaking.

Do You Have Any Recommendations for Tools?

SH: Visual aids? Things like that?

RL: Yes, visual aids.

SH: Well, learning to create a PowerPoint presentation is a good idea.

PowerPoint is a good example, because a lot of us still think of the slide presentations that became known, let's say over the past 30, 40, even 20 years, where you see slides, and there's all these bullet points, and the speaker stands there and kind of, almost reads the bullet points, point for point.

It has come about that that really isn't the best kind of slide presentation there is; that the best speakers put up a slide that might have just an image, a cartoon, it might have a single line on it.

These days, the use of social media, Twitter and Facebook, has become so popular that we're having information quicker, wanting it quicker; to think of Twitter, that limits everything to 140 letters, characters, including spaces; if you think of that when you're creating a slide presentation, no slide should have more than 140 characters, and you could be standing there giving bullet points, but you don't need all of those bullet points on a slide.

You could have a nice handout that the audience can take with them that has those bullet points if they're supposed to be learning from that, but just you as the speaker should still be the center of attention, and what you're saying, and if you're not giving the handout at the right time, that handout could be a distraction from what you're saying.

If you have slides that are not really corresponding to what you're saying, it could be a distraction from your message. So, those visual aids, handouts and slides, posters, signs, PowerPoint presentations, are very valuable.

There is a reason that they're called visual aids: because they're meant to aid the speaker in giving their presentation. So, I would say just, if you're going to go into speaking, learn, any way you can, how to make a good PowerPoint presentation. Learn how to make an animation or cartoon or whatever it is to present your message as an aid rather than presenting the whole message through those aids.

RL: Can you give me a few more examples of how to use them as an aid?

SH: I think I'm gonna just leave it there. I don't know how to give it another example except to say study it a little bit, and learn what's being effective.

One of the ways, well, look at something like TED Talks. They're becoming very popular. What is TED? Technology, education, and design.

But these speakers are coming up and they're giving 18 minute speeches, presentations, and those who are using slides and visual aids are doing it in a way that's not the main focus of their presentation.

It is just being used to enhance their presentation, and that is now known as the most successful way of using visual aids.

Bill Gates of Microsoft gave a presentation at TED Talks a few years back, where he actually wanted to talk about malaria in Africa. You know, he started these foundations to help things.

The way he started his speech is he brought in a jar with some mosquitoes in it, and he took the top off the jar, and he said I just want everyone here to experience malaria from mosquitos the way they're experiencing it in Africa.

Well, believe me, in the first ten seconds of that presentation, he had the audience's attention. That was a visual aid, and the fact was, a little bit into it he said "there's no malaria in these mosquitos, there are a few mosquitoes but there's no malaria," but you get the point.

This is the way people over there are experiencing this. So again, there are ways you can do something that will use as a visual aid of some kind, that can grab someone's attention.

A story is often an aid in the same way. If you can grab that audience's attention and hold it, that audience member is going to remember your message weeks and even months later sometimes, because of that one little added touch you've added to it.

Where do You See Public Speakers Wasting Time When They're Speaking?

SH: Where do I see them wasting time? That's a challenging question. I would say it's often times in not truly having the speech organized when you're getting up there.

If it's been put together a little too quickly, or, how do I put it? It's rambly, it's going on and on, it's maybe repeating things over and over, sometimes it's maybe just not being clear on your message, sometimes it's spending 15 minutes saying something that could've been said in five minutes, it's being repetitive, and I would say that would be one of the things.

Some speakers – and this tends to go with those who are not really in the professional speaking range quite yet – they're learning, they're developing, but if you can see your audience kind of fading away and losing their attention, then that speaker is doing something that isn't quite right to hold and maintain that audience's attention.

It's kind of like the difference between, say, what we might perceive as a teacher in a classroom who's up there just teaching a subject, versus someone who's using speaking skills to entertain and tell stories and grab and maintain that audience' attention. Does that make sense to you?

And I'm not saying also that all teachers are not good speake there are many who are, but it takes a good teacher with g presentation speaking skills to keep a classroom's attention

To be able to teach a subject and not have those kids and those students in class doodling, staring out the window. To really hold their attention, it takes different skills than just reading out of a book.

RL: You said something I might want to expand on a little bit. You said, the speaker's speaking, and the audience starts to wander off. How does the speaker correct when he starts to see that?

SH: For me the word would be impact, and that's doing something that impacts, that grabs that audience's attention. And it can be a joke, it can be something humorous, a story, it can be to subtly yell, it can be to dance across the stage or sing.

ven if you're not a good singer, to suddenly stand there and say
1gs], "if I were the king of the forest," if you think your
ience would look up and say, "Whoa, what happened to this
n? What are they doing?"

e a way to grab their attention back again. Now, typically
should have something to do with the direction you're

o suddenly stand there and juggle, it can be to
gh out loud, it can be to call on a person in the
n be to ask a question that suddenly makes the

s

's;
od

r being a kid in school, and if you weren't
vasn't that when the teacher suddenly said,
u have to say about this?" And you're going

uhhh, and suddenly that teacher has your attention. So maybe it's asking a question, maybe it's making some kind of a scene, but that would be the best way as a speaker to do the same thing, to grab that audience's attention.

RL: So the speaker shouldn't wait; as soon as he sees it, he should fix it.

SH: I would say so, yeah, and it's going to depend on the circumstances and what they're speaking about, but I would say yes.

Probably a part of that problem and the question itself is that most speakers aren't aware of it. I think it's a natural thing for ourselves to be into ourselves, and if you're up on stage, and especially if you're newer and you're developing your skills, you're so busy thinking what do I have to say, what do I have to say next, what is the next story I have to tell, what is the next message I have to give, I want to use the right language, I want to use the right words, and if you have a prepared speech, you don't really want to memorize, but there are certain things you have to kind of know.

I'm telling this story, and then I'm giving this message, and then that goes into this story, and then I want to have this joke, and then I want to call on the audience with these questions, and then I need to come into my conclusion with this other story, and to have that in your mind while you're up there, it's very easy to not be focused enough on your audience, and where are they? Are they giving you their attention? Do you have their attention?

That's part of becoming a better speaker, to be able to see that, to become so comfortable with yourself up there that you're being more natural. That everything about yourself up there is you being you.

You are presenting your very best you, which means it allows you to focus and see what's going on in the audience, which means you're not completely wrapped up in your own mind and what do I have to say and how do I have to say it, and here's how I have to act in this, and here's my joke and I'm remembering this and I have to be that way, because if you're doing that you're not focused on your audience.

So the more you practice the more skillful you become, the more comfortable you become, the better you are able to get up there and focus on serving them, keeping their attention, so that you're able to see okay I've kind of gone off a bit here, I need to come back to my main point, how do I do that? What can I do? Can I clap my hands and sing and dance and get their attention, or what can I do? Ask a question? What can I do to bring this back to where I want their focus?

RL: So it's equally important not just to speak to your audience, but to actually get information from your audience while you're speaking; to involve your audience. How do you do that?

SH: Well those are the things that I've been talking about already. Whether it's, I like to call it grabbing your audience's attention but, to me the first thing and most important is storytelling. Stories people remember.

Stories will draw them in. Stories that keep them on the edge of their seat, and it's that way from children all the way up.

When you can stand there and tell a child an entertaining story and have them sitting on the edge of their seat, you can keep their attention for half an hour by telling a good, suspenseful story, and making them laugh, and keeping them through storytelling.

When there are messages within their story, you can tell the story and then you have the message, and you then repeat the message to the audience.

Zig Ziglar was an expert at that. For anybody who knows Zig Ziglar, he passed away a few years ago, but he was one of the greatest motivational speakers, and he would come up and he would tell a 15 minute story, and at the end of it he would tell a message that he'd just kind of told in the story, and then he would go right from that into his next story.

One story might be about leadership, and you tell a story about this leader and how he led his executives, and then he led his staff, and then he led his employees, and then he led his customers, and at the end of his story he would come back and give the message about leadership, and then he would go right from their into his next story, but his next story might be about being happy, and he would have a story about a woman who's happy at her job and happy at home, and he would have this whole story about the relationship with the kids, and then at the end of it he tells the message that he already said in his story, and then he goes into his next story.

Well, his next story might be about something completely different, about getting water from a well and how you pump the well, and at the end of it, that story is about determination and perseverance to get what you really want in life, and he'll go from one message, to a story, and the stories might not even really relate to each other in the different messages, but that's how he would do it and he was an expert at doing it.

He could stand for two hours and tell story, message, story, message, and that's how he would fill his time.

It's a tactic that I kind of followed, and I like to use when I give a keynote. I'll actually have four or five different messages that I want to present to an audience, so I'll tell four or five different stories, the message, the story, the message, the story, the message. And you can give different messages by giving different stories.

RL: Now in Toastmasters, they have table topics, which is when they call on you with no preparation, versus prepared speeches. What's the difference and purpose of table topics?

SH: Table topics is to teach you improvisational skills, to think on your feet, and there are a number of different purposes for that.

Let's say one, you are a speaker and you're out and something suddenly happens in the audience, or the electricity goes out, or your microphone goes out, or somebody comes charging through the door with some kind of valuable information.

It's being able to think clearly and precisely and be able to deal with it without it being something that stresses you or your audience.

It's being able to deal with it comfortably. But the other thing about improvisational, I like to remind people, that the vast majority of us are going to go out on job interviews. There are those few who maybe got their one job when they were 18 or 21 years old or fresh out of college, and they've never had to go on another interview and they've had one job for 10 years, 20 years, 30 years, and they'll never have to go on another one.

But the vast majority of us nowadays go through different job interviews and different companies, and we work at different jobs, and how many times are you on an interview when suddenly that interviewer asks a question that you're not prepared for?

Richard, if I was to give you this job, and then you got promoted to the manager position, and you had two of your employees who are sitting in office cubicles next to each other and they started an argument, how are you going to diffuse that argument Richard?

Well, suddenly you're on the spot there on an interview, and you're nervous enough because you're on an interview, and you have to answer that question.

Table topics is exactly about that. It's when one person in the room gets up and they ask a question, and then select somebody in the room to stand up for two minutes and answer that question. I tended to find that most beginners in Toastmasters will come in and they'll stand up for 15 or 20 seconds, and then they'll sit down because they've run out of things to say.

Somebody who's been in Toastmasters for five years will stand up and they'll still be able to keep talking after five minutes because we don't learn how to shut up. But it is a skill that's also developed, it's learning to think on your feet.

I've often found in table topics that the question itself can be the challenge for the person who's being asked to speak it.

Some questions can be more fantasy, or fun, or child like, where you have to use your imagination. Some might be more on political, or current extents, or relationships, or could be something that requires a more specific knowledge, or it could be something deeper or more philosophical, and depending on what the questions are, they may be more challenging or easier for that person answering it.

But again, the objective is that no matter what the question is when you're in Toastmasters, you're learning to think quickly on your feet and develop those improvisational skills. It's a great conversational skill to have no matter where you go in your career or in your life. It's part of communication.

Let's even use one more for instance. For a young person who's going off to college, and part of going off to college is having to make new friends and meet new people, you're also coming into an age when you're going to start drinking and going out into the party scene and into the bar scene, and it's kind of nice when you do not have to depend on drinks to be able to loosen yourself up to have a conversation.

But, those social skills alone, to be able to meet somebody, and say it's somebody you're attracted to, a guy who finds a woman attractive or a woman who finds a guy attractive, sometimes that's one of the scariest things in the world.

To go and have a conversation with somebody that you think, wow, I like this person, but what if they reject me? Well, when you develop those skills to be able to have a conversation about almost anything, it's something that people can find attractive.

Of course, you don't want to be the talker and not listen as well, such as I'm doing at this moment, but it is a skill to be able to hold a conversation.

To speak and listen, to speak and listen, and be able to hold a conversation about anything.

If you meet somebody that you find is attractive, and their interest is kayaking and you've never been kayaking, but you still want to be able to show an interest and have a conversation about it, that conversational skill is going to empower you to be able to better impress that person, and that's where table topics and improvisation is going to be able to benefit a person.

RL: Excellent. And another thing I've noticed about Toastmasters is that everything is timed. Why is that?

SH: The biggest reason I'm aware of is if you become a professional speaker, or even if not, let's just say you grow in Toastmasters, you're going to have a time limit on speeches. It could be a 20-minute presentation; it could be a three minute motivational, to get up and you're opening a meeting, and somebody's asked you go come up and give a, what's the world for religious?

RL: Inspirational.

SH: Inspirational might be the word. Just come up and say something inspirational, and you have three minutes. So, you know you have that three minutes.

If you've got ten minutes to speak, or if you develop as a speaker and you have a 20-minute speech, or you have an hour presentation or one and a half hours, there's always a time, and learning to pay attention to that time is very valuable.

If you are a professional speaker and you've been asked to come and speak at a business holiday party. They're having dinner, and they ask you to come for a half an hour while they're eating, they're asking you to come up and speak on something that you have knowledge of but is going to benefit that organization, and maybe relate a little bit to the holidays, and you've got 30 minutes.

To have somebody there that can say, okay 25 minutes have gone by and you have five minutes left, to be prepared ahead of time and say this is how I want to spend these last five minutes, organize your speech for it, is valuable.

Now if you get up there and you're still speaking 45 minutes later, you think that company's ever gonna ask you to come back? Probably not. And same thing, if you get up there and speak for ten minutes and go well, I've run out of things to say, they're probably not going to ask you back either.

So learning to fill that time, and have a well organized presentation, an order or sequence to fill that time, is very important in any kind of speaking engagement, whether it's a 3-minute inspiration, a 20-minute TED Talk, a one hour keynote, or they want you to go speak in front of a board of directors for ten minutes and talk about a new idea that you have. That time is very important and very valuable.

How Important is Good Grammar in Speaking?

SH: I would say that it's very important. That can have various perspectives as well, depending on who your audience is. Let's use a for instance. If you are speaking to a group of engineers, you definitely have to be able to speak their language. Doctors and engineers are kind of recognized for not having the most exciting presentations. They're using a lot of back build and if a person is not quite educated to be able to speak to that audience, they may not be perceived quite as well by the audience.

On the opposite side, if your audience is high school students or even community college, they might not yet be at the higher end of the spectrum.

It's important that your language is appropriate for that audience. The same could even be said if you're called to go and speak at churches, to know who that audience is at church and be able to speak their language.

One might be more Bible fundamentalist and require more of a Bible related message or Bible related stories, where another church might be more in the new age, and more directed toward the empathy of love and spirit and joy and happiness, and you need to be able to speak that language.

We could break it down to the same thing whether you want to talk about ethnicity, races, different languages in different parts of the country, whether you're in New York City or San Francisco, you might have a different type of language you need.

Sometimes an accent might be endearing, sometimes it could actually be difficult to follow and understand if you're out of your element there. So, language has a lot of value in many different ways, whether it's educational level, I would say the main thing is just being able to relate to that audience.

RL: That implies that you need to understand your audience before you walk in the door.

SH: Pretty much. Understand your audience, and understand what it is that they are needing to learn.

In the professional world, there are usually, whether it's in a business or in a speaker's bureau, there is usually a person who is a meeting planner.

They can be the Vice President of the marketing department, they can be human resources person, but for this term we'll call them a meeting planner.

They're the person that you're going to speaking with that is going to be hiring you, or that is requesting that you come speak to their organization, and it might not even be a business.

Let's say you're speaking for the American Businesswoman's Association, and they're having their monthly meeting, and they're asking you to come speak with them.

It's very important that before you even go there, you ask that meeting planner about their audience, and what it is, not only the subject that you would be speaking on, but what is it that they would like to have their audience learn from your presentation?

And then, once again, I brought it up once before, still, get there a half an hour to an hour early, and go and socialize with the people that are going to be in that audience and talk to them a little bit, and just try to grasp a little bit of where they're feeling like they're needing a little bit of direction.

A little help, a little something that you know that might be able to encourage, inspire, assist, direct, suggest, for them. For their improvement, for their betterment, for their development, in their careers, in their lives, in their businesses, whatever it might be.

So yes, knowing your audience and what their needs are is very valuable, and there are a number of ways that you can get that. Whether it's from being part of that audience beforehand, or talking with the meeting planner, talking with executives, anybody who might be associated. Going to websites to learn about the company, anything that you can to get that information, knowing your audience is very valuable.

What About Umms and Ahhs and Sort of's, All the Little Stop Gap Words?

SH: It goes along with the question about language, and using appropriate language.

The average person isn't even aware of the umms and errs and ahhs, but if you're going to become a professional speaker, it is something that you need to learn to improve on, and being in a place like Toastmasters, learning to become a speaker, it's probably one of the first things you start becoming aware of.

How many new Toastmasters in their first meeting stand up and catch themselves saying, and umm oh I caught myself, there's my umm.

I'm going to be honest, I've been in Toastmasters coming up seven years, my very first speech, when I got done, there was somebody in the room that was called the ahhs counter, and they were counting umms and errs and ahhs you say, and when I got done and they gave the report, they said I just stopped counting the umms and errs and ahhs at 20.

So, I learned right away that was something I had to become more aware of, and that's how you improve on it. You become more aware of it.

You start hearing it more and more, being in something like Toastmasters where you're hearing that, you'll start hearing it on television programs, on interviews, on game shows, you'll hear the audience and the people in the game shows doing umms and errs and ahhs.

Even things like the Academy Awards, when these professional actors are being given an award, when they actually have to come up and give their thank you speech, they're not giving a speech usually like memorizing the script and being able to act it out.

They're suddenly coming up there and giving an improvisational thank you, and it's surprising how many umms and errs and ahhs you'll hear.

Politicians, if they're not strongly developed speakers, good communicators, you'll hear them giving umms and errs and ahhs, and there are even other things you'll hear. You'll hear them tapping on the lectern as they're speaking, or you'll see them fidgeting with their clothing or their ties, or just, there's so many little things we learn by being in a group like Toastmasters that you become aware of.

Standing with your hands in your pockets and body language, and how we use our hands and pacing and things like that. There's so many things we do.

There's something called a double clutch, and that's where you use a word over and over. I-I, or like-like, or you know-you know, and it's a way of filling language because you're still trying to develop thoughts and you're speaking through it. So, those are things we learn to improve on.

How Important Are Props in Public Speaking?

SH: I would say that they're important, but that they're not necessary. Some speeches, a prop definitely is going to help.

Let's say you're telling a story about a person trying to catch a cab in New York City, and it's an average looking guy, and he's standing out on the curb, and he's yelling "taxi, taxi, taxi!"

And you said, but I went out there and waved a 20 dollar bill, and yelled taxi, and as soon as I put that 20 dollar bill out, there was a taxi pulling up right at the curb.

Now, even in telling that little story, if you have a 20 dollar bill and you're waving it at your audience, it's going to have a greater impact.

Now, is it necessary to have the 20 dollar bill in your speech? No, but it does help improve and adds impact to your story, and your audience is going to be noticing that 20 dollar bill is waving around there.

So again I would say, having props is not a necessity, but if it's used appropriately, it can enhance the speech and it can enhance the presentation, and it can be very valuable to the speech.

How Would You Develop a Trademark Kind of Speaking Pattern?

SH: I'm not sure what you mean by the trademark, whether you're talking about the creatively inspiring as my tagline, or the subjects that I speak on.

Creatively inspiring to me is just, it's a tagline. It's a way of saying this is my subject matter. Now for me, as I mentioned, I come from a graphic designer and illustrator background, so there's the artist side.

Creativity is part of what I like to have a knowledge of and speaking base about, but how do you speak about creativity and hold an audience's attention to it?

So, I also like motivational, inspirational speaking, which I like to put into entertaining type of formats. And I'll tell you, here are some of the subject matter and direction of some of my most fundamental speeches.

I have one called "Dare to Be Different," and in that case I like to talk about unique people. I like to open with a story about a guy who works in Las Vegas seating people into the taxi cabs as they come out of the hotel, and I talk about how he entertains the people while they're there waiting for the taxi to pull up, and in doing so, he earns far bigger tips than the average person who just stands there and says have a nice day and closes the door behind them, because he's entertaining.

Through that speech, the main message is also that if you think about the most famous people you know; actors, musicians, comedians, inventors, people who have products on shelves; what makes them the top, and the best, and number one in their field?

It's that they're not trying to be like everybody else. Now, we as children were taught to fit in. We were taught that if you're different you're gonna be picked on, you're gonna be kicked back into line by the teachers, you're gonna be told you're different, the other kids are gonna call you weird, and we learn to be average.

But the most successful people and products are those who dare to be different. The best musicians you know and the best bands, they're not trying to be like every other. They may have learned from the others, but they've learned to be unique and they've learned to be different.

The best comedians have learned to develop their own skills. So I like to speak about "Dare to Be Different." I have one called "Grandpa Raymond," in which I actually dress up as a 100 year old man, and when I'm introduced I have the announcer say, "Scott could not be here today, so instead he made a call, and he's got his Grandpa out here, so please welcome Grandpa Raymond," and I come out with the cane.

It's got a horn on it, and I walk down and I tell a story, a life story of being born in 1911 and making it through the Depression and World War II, and having a family and going through a divorce and then getting married a second time, and I bring in all of these elements of life, good and bad, and losing people in my life, and getting through that, and I do it as a 100 plus year old man, and I'm dressed in red polyester pants and a plaid shirt and an ugly tie, and a USS Missouri hat on my head, and right off the bat coming in that way grabs their attention, and I'm able to tell these stories.

I'm also able to tie in messages, and I like to call it carpe diem and seize the day, and I like to talk about overcoming obstacles and having some very emotional stories within the story of life.

So, again, I might say that I'm motivational, inspirational, I'm talking about creativity, but I'm also doing it by showing myself as being a creative person, as taking a part and entertaining and storytelling and having my motivational and inspirational messages within the story, within the speech, within the act, within the whatever it might be.

I've actually done a good half-dozen of those. I've got stories about the power of mind, but I don't just get up and say, "your mind is more powerful than you know!"

Instead I tell a story about each of us having our own spaceship, and how in this spaceship you have your own theatre, and you've got your own control panels, and a holodeck where you can create anything you want. Well, it kind of comes around that this spaceship, you own it, and that it's in your mind.

Well all have that power, and we're not even aware of it. So you do it again by the storytelling, and I have several of those stories in which I'm coming in and entertaining, and taking the part and telling stories and whatever it might be, with a message.

How Would You Handle an Audience That Turns Out to be a Little Hostile?

SH: I can't say that I've had that. The only exception is every now and then I might come in where I'm going to be, instead of being a speaker so to say, I might be what is called an emcee or a host of an event, and usually when I'm hosting an event, I like to come in with some kind of humor using some kind of a joke or something, and sometimes when you open that way, you'll have someone in the audience who, after everybody laughs, they have to yell out their little comment or something like that.

I wouldn't even call it heckling, but you, well there's always somebody who's funny in their own way in the audience and they have to call out some things, and the best I can do is just kind of laugh at it and move on.

It's not something I've really had to deal with. I haven't had anybody that's really treated me badly. I think I'm just unique enough that, again, I should knock on wood here as I'm saying this because now that I'm saying it I'm going to turn around and have somebody that does not like me and is going to make it known to the audience for whatever reason.

I think I seem to remember one of the biggest difficulties I've had, and it's happened a couple of times, where you're called to speak during a group's dinner hour, and maybe you're in a restaurant and the servers are out there putting food on the tables, and you're hearing the clanking of dishes and here you are standing up their trying to grab their attention, and there's people getting food and they're asking can you bring me some ketchup and I'd like this dressing for my salad, and it's just something you have to deal with and kind of realize, this is what I've been asked to do.

I've been asked to speak during this meal. And I've spoken during breakfasts, I've spoken during lunches, I've spoken during dinners, and it's just something you have to deal with, and try your best not to let it bother you. Just realize, because that person is speaking with the server, I can't let it change what I'm doing.

I can't just stop speaking to the rest of them because they're caught up in their thing, and sometimes that happens.

Sometimes you're speaking and somebody else is coming in the door right in the middle of your speech, and you feel like you want to go back and say the first ten minutes of everything you said, because this one person or this couple missed the beginning of it, but you can't do that.

You have to just allow, this is what it is, and just keep moving on and moving forward.

RL: So now I'm curious, on the subject of table topic, in the next two minutes, you're on the holodeck of the USS Enterprise and you can program anything you want, what do you program and why?

SH: For me personally, I would program in some of the success dreams that I have. It's moving myself forward let's say 10 years or 20 years, to where I have achieved my goals and my dreams, and many of my goals and dreams I have achieved in my life. But it comes at different periods, and those goals and dreams change, and they become bigger or they become a new step or whatever it might be.

There are others that I've had all my life, and have never happened yet. So, I think if I really had a holodeck, I would put myself forward to the point of having achieved those goals and dreams, and somehow be able to ask, what did I do to make it happen? How did I get here? [laughter]

And it would maybe make it a little clearer on the steps you have to take to make it happen. I have a lot of strong beliefs about achieving goals and dreams, and a big part of that is taking action to make it happen.

That it's one thing to pray, or to wish, or to hope, but the real successful people are those who take the steps. They're, each day, writing the letter, making the phone call. If you're an author, it's writing another page.

If you're an artist, it's drawing another illustration, another character. If you're a speaker, it's calling this group, it's reaching out to this business, this meeting planner, getting your website done, it's calling the web person to work on the website, it's getting the images together to put on it. It's taking steps, in every part of our life, to be successful.

When you're young, you have a dream of what you want to do and what you want to be, and you kind of have a knowledge that, okay, I need to get through high school, and then I have to go through college to get to this, assuming that you have something professional, and then I have to go to college and I have to get this degree, and then I have to go out and find this first job, and then I have to work my way up through the chain.

Beyond that, we develop other dreams and goals as we go along, but the path to get them isn't always as obvious, and let's say, you know you want to write a book and you want to be a successful author, but how do you become successful? It's one thing to write the book, but then you have to reach out to publishers or you have it self-published, or you want to become a best seller.

How do you get on a *New York Times* bestseller list? How do you get through the social media and things like that? So, we have to go through these steps to learn that process and to make it happen, but it wouldn't it be easier if you could go into your holodeck, and put yourself ten years in the future as already having achieved it all, and being able to say well how did you make that happen?

And then you can go back in time and just take the steps that you've already learned and you already knew you had to take. So to me I think that's what the holodeck would do best for me. It would be to go into the future a little bit and show me exactly what I'd have to do to take the steps to achieve the success that I really want to achieve. Was I two minutes?

RL: No, it was more like four and a half [laughter].

Are There any Books You Would Recommend to Our Audience and Why?

SH: Assuming my audience are people who would like to become professional speakers, one of my favorites is *Talk Like TED*. I brought the book; I don't remember who the author is but I have got the book; but what I especially liked was the audiobook, and I picked it up at the library, and it's, I believe somewhere between 8 or even 9 CDs, and it's all about being a TED Talk speaker.

In case you haven't heard of what TED is, it's Technology, Education, and Design, but there are speakers, and every TED Talk speaker is limited to 18 minutes, and they get up in front of an audience, and most of these presentations are filmed, and they're speaking about a particular subject of their skill and expertise.

And you can go onto YouTube and see a good number of these speeches, but I've found that this book and this audiobook called *Talk like TED* was one of the most valuable I've had as far as great information about all the fundamentals of being a great speaker, and a lot of it relates to being a great TED Talk speaker, but I think most of those fundamentals could be just as valuable in any aspect of speaking.

Several of the others I've had, one that influenced me early on, was called *The Ultimate Handbook of Effective, Persuasive Speaking for Coaches and Leaders*. It was written by Pat Williams with Jim Denny. Pat Williams was once the coach of the Orlando Magic, and I just remember it as being very inspiring to me.

They talked about being a speaker and getting out. There are so many books out there; *Paid to Speak* and *Speak More*, and *Speak and Grow Rich* was a very popular book by Dottie Walters, came out in the nineties, and I believe it was recently updated to include social media, and I believe it was her daughter Lilly Walters who kind of helped update it.

So, there's been several good books. *No Fear Speaking* by Joe Yazbeck is a great book, and I've met Joe and he's a great guy, and also a speaking coach.

Speaking coach is one other subject I'll talk on quickly. If you really want to be a good speaker, I've already said Toastmasters is a place to learn the fundamentals and get your basics in, and I would recommend anybody, get into Toastmasters and stay in it two or three years, to really develop your skills, get your stage time, learn your niche, what you want to speak on, and get your feedback from others, learn all of those fundamentals, and see it almost as though you're going back to college.

But once you've been there for time, let's say two years, if you really want to become a professional speaker, go out and take a look at some of the speaking coaches that are out there.

There are some good ones who really can help you to develop your skills, and especially put you in the direction that's going to be your expertise.

Then, finally there's a group called the National Speakers Association. That is for people who are professional speakers, or they actually have a speaker academy in it for those who want to become professional speakers, and there you're not learning the fundamentals of speaking or developing your speaking skills as much as learning how to become a paid professional speaker, and it's mostly done just by associating with other speakers who are in your field.

So you're more or less getting that association. In Canada they have something called CAPS, it's Canadian Association of Professional Speakers. I'm very good friends with Steve Lowell, who is a speaker coach in Canada, and I think it was 2014 or 2015, he was selected as the speaking coach of the year by CAPS, so getting associated with an organization like that, again, those are the further steps beyond learning the fundamentals of speaking that I would suggest.

It goes along with books, learning, YouTube videos, watching the professional speakers, getting involved with coaches, with other organizations, those are all steps to go further if that's the direction you want to go in to become a professional speaker.

In Closing, Is There Anything You Want to Add?

SH: I think I've rambled quite a bit here. I can't say so. I would just say, if you see yourself as ever becoming any kind of a speaker, just take the steps to do it.

Sometimes the first steps are the hardest, whether you decide to go and do it through a community college and take a public speaking class, or join something like Toastmasters, sometimes that first step, it's to go online, look up Toastmasters, find out where the nearest organizations are.

The three things to look for are a location that's convenient, a time that's convenient, and then go and visit the club. It costs nothing to visit, and even still the membership for Toastmasters is very, very little.

Go there, and go in and see if this is a group of people that you feel like you could become friends with. Each Toastmasters group has a different personality. Some are more professional, and some are more fun, and some are entrepreneurs, and there are corporate Toastmasters clubs within corporations.

So, that hardest part sometimes is getting out of the car and going into a place that you've never been for the first time. It's that lack of familiarity, and it's a little bit of taking a risk, but it isn't a dangerous risk or anything like that. It's just comfort level, and it's one of the first steps you can do in the steps to success.

Make yourself get out of your comfort zone to do something you haven't done. Now, if we're speaking to people who are really wanting to become professional speakers, they've probably already taken some of those first steps, and for that I would say it's the same thing.

Take the next steps. Get the books, go to the National Speaker Association for the first time, look up speaker coaches, look on YouTube for championship speakers, professional speakers.

Look at Tony Robbins and Jack Canfield and Wayne Dyer, or the leadership speaker Brian Tracy, or whoever it might be, and start learning.

Learn all you can, and start reaching out to businesses, and let them know you're a professional speaker. Get a business card that says professional speaker on it.

When you do that, if you feel like you can't put your name on a business card that says professional speaker, then you need to get to where you can, and that's the first part. It's taking that first step to feel comfortable yourself, and just take steps.

That's gonna be my word. Just take the step, keep taking the steps, one step at a time.

Closing

RL: Thank you, **Scott Howard**, for a great interview. I'm sure all the **public speakers** in our audience will have a much better understanding of the necessary skills needed for **public speaking** now that you've laid everything out so clearly. Thank you so much for sharing your expertise and experiences so graciously.

Can you tell me a little bit more about your website, scotthowardspeaks.com, and how does it help public speakers with speaking?

SH: Actually, it's kind of funny, but right at this time it's down. I've got it down because I'm redoing and updating the website, but it's actually more about my direction as a speaker than so much providing public speaking skills.

It's my way of introducing my niche, creatively inspiring, who I am, saying that I do keynote speaking, that I do workshops, and that I also do hosting and emceeing for events. There are different directions that speakers can go in, and generally we have to pick our niches, and that's how I use my website.

You're asking me this question actually makes me think, gee, maybe I should have a little bit more on it about becoming a professional speaker. There's a pretty big audience out there of people who are, I shouldn't even call it an audience.

There are speaker coaches, there are groups and organizations, there are people who put on workshops for speakers, and they almost all have websites that talk about how to become professional speakers.

For me, I haven't really gone in that direction except within the Toastmasters organization to help newer Toastmasters to develop and become better speakers, and develop their skills and develop the fundamentals.

Maybe it's something I could go into a little bit more, but for now I'm trying to develop as a professional speaker myself, and get more paid speaking gigs I guess is the word.

So I'm doing a lot more locally, and would probably like to be out more nationally, and even internationally, and do some travelling and develop my name even more. So that's where

I'm going with redeveloping my website right now is showing more of who I am, and then once it's redeveloped I'm ready to point more potential clients to it, and show some of my videos of my own speeches, things like that. So that's where I'm going.

RL: Thank you. And thank you again for speaking with us, and thank you to the public speakers out there in the audience for joining us for this amazing presentation about skills everyone needs to succeed in public speaking.

I'm Richard Lowe, and thanks again for joining us in the *Interviews with Influence* e-book series.

SH: Richard I thank you for having me on here today. I'm honored to even be in your presence. You're awesome.

RL: Have a great day! That was fun.

Before you go

If you scroll to the last page in this eBook, you will have the opportunity to leave feedback and share the book with Before You Go. I'd be grateful if you turned to the last page and shared the book.

Also, if you have time, please leave a review on Amazon. Positive reviews are incredibly useful. If you didn't like the book, please email me at rich@thewritingking.com and I'd be happy to get your input.

Creatively Inspiring' Scott Howard

In the Creative World, Scott Howard is well recognized as a successful graphic designer and illustrator. His first book, the amazing, one-of-a-kind "Artsy Ant Alphabet Art Adventures" increased Scott's recognition as a creative artist, imaginative storyteller, and influential thought leader, educating and encouraging kids, and 'Creatively Inspiring' all ages!

A dynamic speaker, Scott has become recognized for entertaining and 'Creatively Inspiring' stories, such as "Dare To Be Different," "Grandpa Raymond," "Planet Happy" and "Remember What it's Like to be a Kid", with messages related to the Power of Our Minds, Seize the Day, Being our Most Awesome Selves, Creativity, Creative Thinking, and Public Speaking.

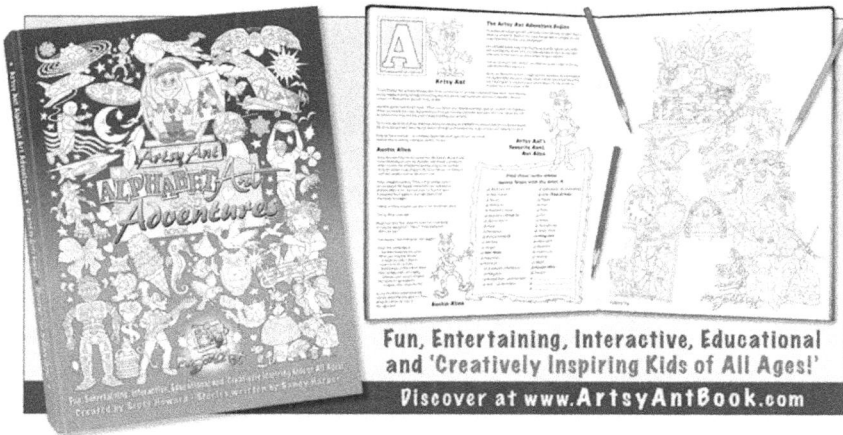

Fun, Entertaining, Interactive, Educational and 'Creatively Inspiring Kids of All Ages!'
Discover at www.ArtsyAntBook.com

Scott often appears as a Children's Book Author and Speaker at children's charities and events. His greatest joy is in encouraging confidence in children to follow their passions, achieve their dreams, and to live their best lives.

Storytelling with kids of all ages includes imaginative tales such as "The Enchanting Camping Trip," and Artsy Ant book stories. Question & Answer sessions empower kids to believe in themselves, their careers, and guide them toward a more positive future.

Born in Claremont New Hampshire, Scott grew up in Rehoboth, Massachusetts. He served as a graphic artist and illustrator with the US Army, received an Associate's degree at Monterey Peninsula College, and Bachelor of Arts degree at California State University in Fullerton, California. Scott currently lives in Tampa Bay, Florida. He is a proud, long-time member of Toastmasters and CEOSpace, and enjoys several other business professional networking groups.

Websites:

www.ArtsyAntBook.com
www.MyScottArt.com
www.ScottHowardSpeaks.com

Email: Scott@MyScottArt.com

About the Author

https://www.linkedin.com/in/richardlowejr
Feel free to send a connection request

Follow me on Twitter: @richardlowejr

Richard Lowe has leveraged more than 35 years of experience as a Senior Computer Manager and Designer at four companies into that of a bestselling author, blogger, ghostwriter, and public speaker. He has written hundreds of articles for blogs and ghostwritten more than a dozen books and has published manuscripts about computers, the Internet, surviving disasters, management, and human rights. He is currently working on a ten-volume science fiction series – the Peacekeeper Series – to be published at the rate of three volumes per year, beginning in 2016.

Richard started in the field of Information Technology, first as the Vice President of Consulting at Software Techniques, Inc. Because he craved action, after six years he moved on to work for two companies at the same time: he was the Vice President of Consulting at Beck Computer Systems and the Senior Designer at BIF Accutel. In January 1994, Richard found a home at Trader Joe's as the Director of Technical Services and Computer Operations. He remained with that incredible company for almost 20 years before taking an early retirement to begin a new life as a professional writer. He is currently the CEO of The Writing King, a company that provides all forms of writing services, the owner of The EBay King, and a Senior Branding Expert for LinkedIn Makeover. You can find a current list of all books on his Author Page and take a look at his exclusive line of coloring books at The Coloring King.

Richard has a quirky sense of humor and has found that life is full of joy and wonder. As he puts it, "This little ball of rock, mud, and water we call Earth is an incredible place, with many secrets to discover. Beings fill our corner of the universe, and some are happy, and others are sad, but each has their unique story to tell."

His philosophy is to take life with a light heart, and he approaches each day as a new source of happiness. Evil is ignored, discarded, or defeated; good is helped, enriched, and fulfilled. One of his primary interests is to educate people about their human rights and assist them to learn how to be happy in life.

Richard spent many happy days hiking in national parks, crawling over boulders, and peering at Indian pictographs. He toured the

Channel Islands off Santa Barbara and stared in fascination at wasps building their homes in Anza-Borrego. One of his joys is photography, and he has photographed more than 1,200 belly dancing events, as well as dozens of Renaissance fairs all over the country.

Because writing is his passion, Richard remains incredibly creative and prolific; each day he writes between 5,000 and 10,000 words, diligently using language to bring life to the world so that others may learn and be entertained.

Richard is the CEO of The Writing King, which specializes in fulfilling any writing need. You can find out more at https://www.thewritingking.com/, and emails are welcome at rich@thewritingking.com

Books by Richard G Lowe Jr.

Business Professional Series

On the Professional Code of Ethics and Business Conduct in the Workplace – Professional Ethics: 100 Tips to Improve Your Professional Life - have you ever wondered what it takes to be successful in the professional world? This book gives you some tips that will improve your job and your career.

Help! My Boss is Whacko! - How to Deal with a Hostile Work Environment - sometimes the problem is the boss. There are all kinds of managers, some competent, some incompetent, and others just plain whacked. This book will help you understand and handle those different types of managers.

Help! I've Lost My Job: Tips on What to do When You're Unexpectedly Unemployed – suddenly having to leave your job can be a harsh and emotional time in your life. Learn some of the things that you need to consider and handle if this happens to you.

Help! My Job Sucks Insider Tips on Making Your Job More Satisfying and Improving Your Career – sometimes conditions conspire to make the regular trek to a job feel like a trip through Dante's Inferno. Sometimes, these are out of our control, such as a malicious manager or incompetent colleague. On the other hand, we can take control of our lives and workplace and improve our situation. Get this book to learn what you can do when your job sucks.

How to Manage a Consulting Project: Make money, get your project done on time, and get referred again and again – I found that being a consultant is a great way to earn a living. Managing a consulting project can be a challenge. This book contains some tips to help you so you can deliver a better product or service to your customers.

How to be a Good Manager and Supervisor, and How to Delegate – Lessons Learned from the Trenches: Insider Secrets for Managers and Supervisors – I've been a manager for over thirty years I learned many things about how to get the job done and deliver quality service. The information in this book will help you manage your projects to a high level of quality.

Focus on LinkedIn – Learn how to create a LinkedIn profile and to network effectively using the #1 business social media site.

Home Computer Security Series

Safe Computing is Like Safe Sex: You have to practice it to avoid infection – Security expert and Computer Executive, Richard Lowe, presents the simple steps you can take to protect your computer, photos and information from evil doers and viruses. Using easy-to-understand examples and simple explanations, Lowe explains why hackers want your system, what they do with your information, and what you can do to keep them at bay. Lowe answers the question: how to you keep yourself say in the wild west of the internet.

Disaster Preparation and Survival Series

Real World Survival Tips and Survival Guide: Preparing for and Surviving Disasters with Survival Skills – CERT (Civilian Emergency Response Team) trained and Disaster Recovery Specialist, Richard Lowe, lays out how to make you, your family, and your friends ready for any disaster, large or small. Based upon specialized training, interviews with experts and personal experience, Lowe answers the big question: what is the secret to improving the odds of survival even after a big disaster?

Creating a Bug Out Bag to Save Your Life: What you need to pack for emergency evacuations - When you are ordered to evacuate—or leave of your free will—you probably won't have a lot of time to gather your belongings and the things you'll need. You may have just a few minutes to get out of your home. The best preparation for evacuation is to create what is called a bug out bag. These are also known as go-bags, as in, "grab it and go!"

Professional Freelance Writer Series

How to Operate a Freelance Writing Business, and How to be a Ghostwriter – Proven Tips and Tricks Every Author Needs to Know about Freelance Writing: Insider Secrets from a Professional Ghostwriter – This book explains how to be a ghostwriter, and gives tips on everything from finding customers to creating a statement of work to delivering your final product.

How to Write a Blog That Sells and How to Make Money From Blogging: Insider Secrets from a Professional Blogger: Proven Tips and Tricks Every Blogger Needs to Know to Make Money – There is an art to writing an article that prompts the reader to make a decision to do something. That's the narrow focus of this book. You will learn how to create an article that gets a reader interested, entices them, informs them, and causes them to make a decision when they reach the end.

Additional Resources

Is your career important to you? Find out how to move your career in any direction you desire, improve your long-term livelihood, and be prepared for any eventuality. Visit the page below to sign up to receive valuable tips via email, and to get a free eBook about how to optimize your LinkedIn profile.

http://list.thewritingking.com/

I've written and published many books on a variety of subjects. They are all listed on the following page.

https://www.thewritingking.com/books/

On that site, I also publish articles about business, writing, and other subjects. You can visit by clicking the following link:

https://www.thewritingking.com

To find out more about me or my photography, you can visit these sites:

Personal website: https://www.richardlowe.com
Photography: http://www.richardlowejr.com
LinkedIn Profile: https://www.linkedin.com/in/richardlowejr
Twitter: https://twitter.com/richardlowejr

If you have any comments about this book, feel free to email me at rich@thewritingking.com

Premium Writing Services

Do you have a story that needs to be told? Have you been trying to write a book for ages but never can seem to find the time to get it done? Do you want to brand your business, but don't know how to get started?

The Writing King has the answer. We can help you with any of your writing needs.

Ghostwriting. We can write your book, which entails interviewing you to get your story, writing the book and then working with you to revise it until complete. To discuss your book, contact The Writing King today.

Website Copy. Many businesses include the text on their sites as an afterthought, and that can result in lost sales and leads. Hire The Writing King to review your site and recommend changes to the text which will help communicate your message and improve your sales.

Blogging. Build engagement with your customers by hiring us to write a weekly or semi-weekly article for your blog, LinkedIn or other social media. Contact The Writing King today to discuss your blogging needs.

LinkedIn. LinkedIn is of the most important vehicles for finding new business, and a professionally written profile works to pulling in those leads. Write or update your profile today.

Technical Writing. We have broad experience in the computer, warehousing and retail industries, and have written hundreds of technical documents. Contact The Writing King today to find out how we can help you with your technical writing project.

The Writing King has the skills and knowledge to help you with any of your writing needs. Call us today to discuss how we can help you.

www.ingramcontent.com/pod-product-compliance
Lightning Source LLC
Chambersburg PA
CBHW071500210326
41597CB00018B/2638

Other Books by Richard Lowe Jr

How to Be Friends with Women: How to Surround Yourself with Beautiful Women without Being Sleazy – I am a photographer and frequently find myself surrounded by some of the most beautiful women in the world. This book explains how men can attract women and keep them as friends, which can often lead to real, fulfilling relationships.

How to Throw Parties like a Professional: Tips to Help You Succeed with Putting on a Party Event – Many of us have put on parties, and I know it can be a daunting and confusing experience. In this book, I share what I learned from hosting small house parties to shows and events.